THE ULTIMATE BOOK OF HOLIDAY KID CONCOCTIONS

More Than 50 Wacky, Wild, & Crazy Concoctions for All Occasions

John E. & Danita Thomas

B&H
PUBLISHING GROUP

Nashville, Tennessee

rdi

Dedications

We would like to dedicate this book to our children:
Kyle, Kalie, Kellen, and Christian who inspire us
each day to keep concocting!

Acknowledgments

We would also like to thank the parents, grandparents, educators, and others who have used Kid Concoctions to enrich the life of a child.

Foreword

Among the childhood treasures that we keep throughout our lives are fond and happy memories of holidays spent with family and friends. We hope *The Ultimate Book of Holiday Kid Concoctions* will provide you with a wealth of ideas for creating wonderful traditions and memories with the children in your life. In this book you will find fun, easy-to-make, inexpensive projects along with creative tips to make your holidays even more special.

Every holiday is a wonderful opportunity to celebrate the traditions, values, and morals that are important in your life. As people of strong faith, it is our desire that this book bless families from all religions and cultures while celebrating the family. We encourage you to take the opportunity during fun and creative play to pass on your family traditions and beliefs to your children.

We have included many holidays and festive occasions. If you celebrate a holiday that is not found in these pages, be creative and use some of the fun activities in this book to help make your holiday even more special.

May God bless you and your family. Happy holiday concocting!

John E. Thomas & Danita Thomas

CONTENTS

Adult supervision is recommended for all projects and recipes.

NEW YEAR'S

New Year's Eve is a time to celebrate the passing of one year and the birth of another. Although many cultures observe this holiday at different times, the beginning of a new year is always cause for celebration.

Tips for a great New Year's celebration:

Make it a tradition to spend this time as a family. If you go out on New Year's Eve, then schedule your family time on New Year's Day. Family games or a night at the movies is a great way to begin your evening celebration.

Have everyone write down their goals and dreams for the New Year and hide them in a secret place until next year's celebration. It's fun to see how many came true.

Look through family photos from the past year together. Sing and dance along with the entertainers on the television countdowns. Bang on pots and pans outside and cheer with excitement at midnight.

NEW YEAR'S NOISEMAKERS

This homemade noisemaker is a perfect way to bring in the New Year.

WHAT YOU WILL NEED:

2 clear plastic cups
1/4 cup mixed dried beans, rice, and macaroni
Colored tape

HOW TO CONCOCT IT:

1. Pour dried beans, rice, and macaroni into one clear plastic cup.
2. Place the other plastic cup on top of the first cup
   so they are rim to rim.
3. Securely tape the two cups together and shake.

CONCOCTION TIPS & IDEAS:

◆ Decorate the outside of your New Year's Noisemakers with markers
   or construction paper.
◆ Jazz up your Noisemakers by adding a little bit of glitter or confetti.

PARTY WANDS

Use Party Wands to bring in the New Year with an explosion of glitter and confetti.

WHAT YOU WILL NEED:
Paper towel tube
Confetti
Construction paper
Markers
Clear tape
Glitter

HOW TO CONCOCT IT:
1. Cover one end of the paper towel tube with tape.
2. Decorate the tube with New Year's Eve designs using markers, construction paper, and clear tape.
3. Fill the tube with confetti.
4. Wad up a piece of paper and place it in the open end of the tube to keep the glitter and confetti in place.
5. Just before midnight, remove the wad of paper. When the clock strikes midnight, wave the Party Wands in the air to create an explosion of confetti.

CONCOCTION TIPS & IDEAS:
◆ Add glitter and thin streamers to your Party Wands.
◆ Fill your Party Wands with treats and pieces of candy.

CONFETTI BALLOONS

This New Year's Eve party favor will explode into a cloud of confetti.

WHAT YOU WILL NEED:

1 large balloon
1/4 cup paper confetti
Toothpick
Funnel

HOW TO CONCOCT IT:

1. Pull the balloon over the end of the funnel.
2. Pour confetti into the balloon.
3. Remove the balloon from the funnel and blow it up being careful not to get any confetti in your mouth.
4. Tie the balloon shut.
5. When the clock hits midnight yell, "Happy New Year!" Hold the Confetti Balloon away from your face and pop it with a toothpick.

CONCOCTION TIPS & IDEAS:

◆ Write a New Year's message on a piece of paper. Roll it up and place it in the balloon before blowing it up.
◆ Use felt-tip markers to decorate the outside of your Confetti Balloons.

VALENTINE'S DAY

Valentine's Day is the day each year set aside to celebrate the love we have for our friends, family, and sweethearts. It is often celebrated with the exchange of fancy cards, flowers, and candy.

Tips for a special Valentine's Day:

Make a special Valentine's Day flower bouquet. Get white carnations and place them in a mixture of red food coloring and water. It is fun to watch the magical transformation as the white flowers suddenly become tipped in red.

Serve a meal with red napkins and heart-shaped white lace doilies that you can find at your local craft store. Place a homemade heart place card at everyone's seat and have a candlelight dinner.

Have each family member make a valentine for other members telling each person one thing they really like about them. This can be fun with friends too.

SWEETHEART CHOCOLATE ROSES

These Sweetheart Chocolate Roses are not only beautiful to look at but also good to eat!

WHAT YOU WILL NEED:

Bag of small chocolate kisses
Red or pink plastic wrap
Green tape
Clear tape
Green pipe cleaners
Green tissue paper

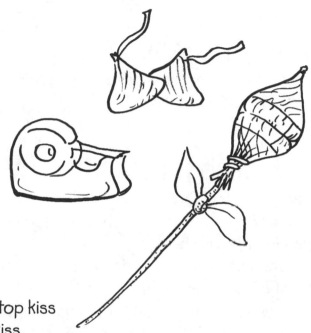

HOW TO CONCOCT IT:

1. First make your rose bud by taping two, foil-wrapped kisses together end to end with plastic tape.
2. Cut and drape a 5-inch square of plastic wrap over the point of the top kiss and gather the edges twisting into a tail at the point of the bottom kiss.
3. Twist the top of a green pipe cleaner around the tail to form a stem.
4. Add leaves by twisting the pipe cleaner once around the center of a green strip of tissue paper.
5. Cut each end of the tissue paper strip so that the tissue paper resembles rose leaves. Repeat the above steps several times to make a bouquet of Sweetheart Chocolate Roses.

CONCOCTION TIPS & IDEAS:

◆ Arrange several Sweetheart Chocolate Roses in a vase with real greens and give it as a Valentine's Day gift.
◆ Use different colors of plastic wrap to create a bouquet of roses in assorted colors.

COOKIE BOUQUET

Instead of giving your loved one a bouquet of flowers, why not try giving this fun-to-make Cookie Bouquet.

WHAT YOU WILL NEED:
1 package (18 ounces) refrigerated chocolate chip cookie dough
8 flat, wooden sticks

HOW TO CONCOCT IT:

1. Preheat oven to 375 degrees.
2. Roll the dough into eight, 2-inch balls. Place the balls on an ungreased cookie sheet.
3. Insert the wooden sticks into each ball so they look like a lollipop. Slightly flatten the dough.
4. Bake 13 to 15 minutes or until the edges of the cookies are crisp.
5. Ask an adult to help take the cookies out of the oven and transfer the cookies to a wire rack. Allow them to cool completely.
6. Put your cookies together to form a bouquet and give as a gift.

CONCOCTION TIPS & IDEAS:
◆ Jazz up your Cookie Bouquet by tying a red ribbon around each stick and then wrap the cookie in plastic colored wrap.
◆ Arrange your Cookie Bouquet in a small glass vase or floral box just like you would a bouquet of flowers.

GIANT CHOCOLATE KISS

Make a Giant Chocolate Kiss just like the ones you buy in the store. That's bound to put a smile on anyone's face.

WHAT YOU WILL NEED:

1 bag of milk chocolate chips
Round funnel
Coffee mug
Nonstick spray
Foil

HOW TO CONCOCT IT:

1. Melt the chocolate chips in the microwave or in a double boiler.
2. Place some foil over the small end of a funnel.
3. Place the funnel upright in a coffee mug. Spray the funnel with nonstick cooking spray.
4. Pour the melted chocolate into the funnel and place it in the freezer for 45 minutes or until the chocolate has hardened completely.
5. Remove the chocolate from the funnel and wrap it in foil.
6. Write a message on a narrow piece of paper. Tuck the end of it into the foil at the point of the kiss.

CONCOCTION TIPS & IDEAS:

◆ This project requires the assistance and supervision of an adult.
◆ This project can also be made using white chocolate chips and peanut butter chips.
◆ Try wrapping red plastic wrap over the foil for an even more festive look.

ST. PATRICK'S DAY

This holiday pays tribute to St. Patrick, the patron saint of Ireland, and was originally celebrated by people of Irish descent. Shamrocks and the color green are the most common symbols of St. Patrick's Day.

Tips for a fun St. Patrick's Day:

Draw a little shamrock on the back of your hand or on your cheek with a washable nontoxic marker.

Dress in green from head to toe.

For a fun drink, add a few drops of green food coloring to your milk. You can also add green food coloring to other foods like scrambled eggs, cake icing, mashed potatoes, pancakes, or anything else you can think of.

SHAMROCK GLASS COOKIES

Celebrate St. Patrick's Day with these cookies that look like stained glass and taste like candy.

WHAT YOU WILL NEED:

1 package of premade sugar cookie dough
Green hard candy (Life Savers or Jolly Ranchers)
Plastic ziplock bags
Rolling pin
2 shamrock shaped cookie cutters (1 large and 1 small)

HOW TO CONCOCT IT:

1. Roll out cookie dough and cut out cookies using the large shamrock cookie cutter. Using the small shamrock cookie cutter, cut a hole in the center of each cookie.
2. Place cookies on a foil covered cookie sheet.
3. Put hard candies in a ziplock bag and crush them using the rolling pin.
4. Use the crushed candy to fill the holes in the center of the cookies.
5. Get an adult to help you bake your cookies at 375 degrees for 8 to 10 minutes until lightly brown. Cool completely and then peel the cookies off the foil.

CONCOCTION TIPS & IDEAS:

◆ Make this project using other holiday-shaped cookie cutters and colored candies (e.g., heart-shaped cookie cutters and red candy for Valentine's Day).

LEPRECHAUN'S LUCKY SHAKE

Children and Leprechauns of all ages will enjoy this minty ice cold shake.

WHAT YOU WILL NEED:

1 cup milk
1 scoop vanilla ice cream
2 ice cubes
Mint extract to taste
Food coloring

HOW TO CONCOCT IT:

1. Place milk, ice cream, and ice cubes in a blender and blend on high for 10 seconds.
2. Add 3 to 4 drops of mint extract and 2 drops of green food coloring, blending for an additional 10 seconds.
3. Pour Leprechaun's Lucky Shake into a glass and serve.

CONCOCTION TIPS & IDEAS:

◆ Spice up your shake by adding a little whipped cream and a cherry on top.
◆ Give your shake a little zing by adding a splash of seltzer water.

EMERALD ISLE SHAMROCK

This living shamrock will delight adults and amaze children as it grows.

WHAT YOU WILL NEED:

Potting soil
Quick growing grass seed
Pencil
Pie tin
Plant mister

HOW TO CONCOCT IT:

1. Fill a pie tin with a 3-inch layer of potting soil.
2. Spray a light layer of water over the soil with a plant mister.
3. Use a pencil to draw a picture of a shamrock in the moist soil.
4. Sprinkle a thin layer of grass seed inside your shamrock and cover with a
   1/4-inch layer of soil. Mist with water.
5. Place your Emerald Isle Shamrock in a sunny window and mist with water 1 to 2 times a day.
   The seeds will begin to sprout in just a few days.

CONCOCTION TIPS & IDEAS:

◆ Try using other types of seeds like herb seeds.
◆ Draw a picture of a Christmas tree in the soil and grow a living tree during the Christmas season.

EASTER

Easter is a Christian holiday that celebrates the rebirth of Christ. Bunnies, colored eggs, baby chicks, and lilies are often used as symbols of this holiday.

Tips for a Happy Easter:

Use the Kid Concoctions' Treasure Stones dough recipe found on page 15 to cover your treat-filled plastic eggs. It will make your Easter egg hunt much more challenging and fun.

Have a family egg hunt with plastic eggs filled with coupons from Mom or Dad that have special rewards or privileges on them. Some of our family favorites are: You don't have to make your bed today; You can stay up one half-hour past bedtime; Mom will clean your room today; I owe you one dollar.

If your family celebrates Easter, attend a church service together. Read the story of Easter as a family and then discuss.

MYSTERY MESSAGE EGGS

Family and friends will have fun breaking open real eggs with hidden messages inside.

WHAT YOU WILL NEED:

Eggs
Toothpick or straight pin
Paper
Colored markers
Turkey baster

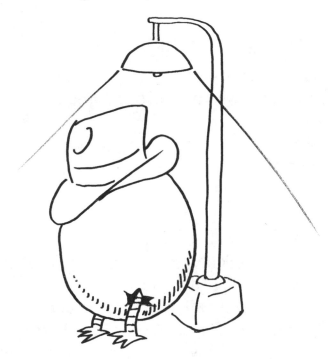

HOW TO CONCOCT IT:

1. Use a toothpick or straight pin to poke a small hole in one end of an egg and a large hole in the other end.
2. Use a turkey baster to suck out the contents of the egg through the large hole.
3. Carefully rinse the eggshell out with soap and water. Shake excess water out of the eggshell and allow it to dry.
4. Carefully decorate your eggshells with colored markers or with the Quick & Easy Egg Dye recipe on page 25.
5. Write messages on small pieces of paper. Roll up the message and place it in the egg through the large hole.

CONCOCTION TIPS & IDEAS:

◆ Paint designs on your Mystery Message Eggs using a mixture of 3 to 4 drops of food coloring to 1 Tbs. water.
◆ Put dollar bills in your mystery eggs and hide them in the backyard for the ultimate egg hunt.

LIVING BASKET

Celebrate this holiday of rebirth by growing your very own basket of Easter grass.

WHAT YOU WILL NEED:

Colored plastic wrap
Grass seed (wheat seed or rye seed)
Potting soil
Basket
Plant mister

HOW TO CONCOCT IT:

1. Line the basket with plastic wrap, leaving a one-inch lip hanging over the side of the basket.
2. Fill the basket with 3 to 4 inches of soil.
3. Sprinkle a fine layer of grass seed over the soil and then cover the grass seed with 1/4-inch of potting soil. Spray with plant mister.
4. Place the basket in a warm, sunny window and spray the soil with a plant mister 2 to 3 times a day. After 4 or 5 days your grass will begin to sprout. You should have a beautiful basket of grass in 2 to 3 weeks.

CONCOCTION TIPS & IDEAS:

◆ Plant some flower seeds in your Living Basket and give it to a friend or family member as a gift.
◆ Decorate your basket with ribbon and fill it with beautiful Easter eggs to make the perfect Easter dinner centerpiece.

QUICK & EASY EGG DYE

This concoction lets you create beautiful colored eggs in minutes.

WHAT YOU WILL NEED:
1 Tbs. food coloring
1 Tbs. vinegar
Hard-boiled eggs
Water

HOW TO CONCOCT IT:
1. Combine food coloring and vinegar in
   a small bowl until blended.
2. Add enough water to make the liquid deep enough
   to cover an egg.
3. Swirl the liquid around with a spoon. Quickly lower an egg into the
   solution and remove.
4. Pat the egg dry with a paper towel.
5. Put a little bit of cooking oil on a paper towel and rub the egg with it.
   This will give the egg a varnished look.

CONCOCTION TIPS & IDEAS:
◆ Draw a design on your egg with a white crayon before dipping. The dye will not stick to your design.
◆ Make different colors of egg dye. Dip one half of the egg in one color and the other half in another color.

EGGHEAD GUYS

This wild and crazy garden concoction is a fun way to celebrate Easter.

WHAT YOU WILL NEED:

Eggs
Potting soil
Grass seeds, flower seeds, or herb seeds
Felt-tip markers
Egg carton
Plant mister

HOW TO CONCOCT IT:

1. Hollow out the eggs by tapping the small end against a hard surface to create a 1-inch hole on top of the egg.
2. Remove the contents of the egg by carefully shaking it over a bowl and carefully rinse the egg.
3. Carefully draw a face on the egg using felt-tip markers or face paint.
4. Spoon each egg full of potting soil and make a small hole in the soil with a pencil.
5. Place a few seeds in the hole and cover the seeds with soil. Lightly spray with plant mister. Put the planted eggs in the egg carton and place the egg carton in a sunny window. Mist the planted eggs every day or so. Depending on the type of seeds used, your Egghead Garden will sprout in 7 to 10 days.

CONCOCTION TIPS & IDEAS:

◆ Transplant your Egghead Garden outside and enjoy it all summer.
◆ Use feathers and ears cut out of paper to make your eggs look like rabbits and chickens.

CINCO DE MAYO

A festival of Hispanic heritage celebrated with mariachi music, folkloric dancing, and Mexican food.

Tips for a super Cinco de Mayo celebration:

Decorate your kitchen and prepare a Mexican meal.

Learn Spanish words by making special flash cards.

Wear a *sombrero* (Mexican hat) and a *sarape* (shawl worn over one shoulder) even if you have to make your own out of things you have around the house.

Play some Mexican music or sing Mexican songs and have a *fiesta*. (Party!)

CINCO DE MAYO CORN CHIPS

Children will be amazed they can make these delicious corn chips at home.

WHAT YOU WILL NEED:

1/2 cup yellow cornmeal
1/2 tsp. salt
1 cup very hot water
3/4 cup very hot water
1 tsp. margarine

HOW TO CONCOCT IT:

1. Mix cornmeal and salt together in a large bowl.
2. Pour in one cup of very hot water and margarine, stir until margarine is melted.
3. Add 3/4 cup of very hot water and stir.
4. Drop spoonfuls of the corn chip mixture onto a greased cookie sheet.
5. Bake at 450 degrees for 12 to 15 minutes or until golden brown.
   Get an adult to help you with the oven.

CONCOCTION TIPS & IDEAS:

◆ Add a few drops of food coloring to your Cinco de Mayo Corn Chips to make a colorful and tasty bowl of chips.

QUICK & EASY SALSA

This classic homemade salsa tastes great and is very easy to make.

WHAT YOU WILL NEED:

2 to 3 medium tomatoes, chopped
1/2 cup chopped onion
4 to 6 chilies serranos (jalapenos can be substituted)
1/3 cup chopped cilantro
1 tsp. salt
Juice from one-quarter fresh lime

HOW TO CONCOCT IT:

1. Mix all of the ingredients together in a small bowl.
2. Cover the mixture and let it sit for one hour before serving.

CONCOCTION TIPS & IDEAS:

◆ Serve Quick & Easy Salsa with Cinco de Mayo Corn Chips for a tasty snack.

PARTY PIÑATA

This classic papier-mâché concoction recipe has been a favorite of children for many years.

WHAT YOU WILL NEED:

1 cup cold water
1/4 cup flour
5 cups water
Large, blown-up balloon
Long, narrow newspaper strips

HOW TO CONCOCT IT:

1. Mix flour and 1 cup of water in a small bowl until smooth.
2. With adult help heat 5 cups of water in a large saucepan over Medium heat until the water begins to boil.
3. Also with adult help add flour and water mixture to boiling water. Continue to boil, while stirring constantly for 3 to 5 minutes.
4. Remove pan from heat and allow papier-mâché paste to cool.
5. Dip strips of newspaper in papier-mâché paste and place them over the blown-up balloon, leaving a small hole at the top. This hole needs to be just big enough to accommodate candy and small gifts. Place several layers of papier-mâché newspaper strips over the balloon so that your piñata is sturdy.
6. After the newspaper strips have dried, pop the balloon and fill the empty cavity with candy and toy prizes. Seal the hole with duct tape and decorate the piñata with paint, colored markers, streamers, and crepe paper.

CONCOCTION TIPS & IDEAS:

◆ Suspend the piñata and take turns with your friends, trying to hit it with a stick while blindfolded. Eventually, the piñata will break open, releasing the candy and toy prizes.
◆ Party Piñatas are also great for birthday parties and other celebrations.

MOTHER'S DAY

Mother's Day is a holiday celebrated in the United States on the second Sunday in May. On Mother's Day, children show their love and appreciation for their mothers by honoring them with gifts, flowers, and cards.

Tips to make Mother's Day even more special:

Give Mom a fresh bouquet of flowers. The flowers children pick for their mothers in their own yard are just as special as the ones bought in the store.

Write Mom a love letter; she will keep it for a very long time.

Make coupons for Mom of things you will do to help her around the house. Moms can always use a cheerful helper.

Start Mom's special day by serving her juice, coffee, or even breakfast in bed.

BEAUTY BATH SALTS

Mom will love taking a nice relaxing bath in Beauty Bath Salts you can make yourself.

WHAT YOU WILL NEED:

1 clear plastic peanut butter jar (clean with the label removed)
2 cups Epsom salt
1 cup coarse salt
Food coloring
Perfume or essential oil (for fragrance)

HOW TO CONCOCT IT:

1. Mix both kinds of salt together in a bowl. Add 2 to 3 drops of food coloring and mix.
2. Add 5 to 6 drops of perfume or essential oil and stir.
3. Spoon the mixture into a jar and screw on the lid.
4. Make a gift tag with the name of the fragrance used and directions that suggest using 1/3 to 1/2 cup of Beauty Bath Salts in the bathtub.

CONCOCTION TIPS & IDEAS:

◆ Layer different colors of salt in the plastic jar to create a sand art effect.
◆ Decorate the top of your jar by placing a small square of fabric over it and then secure the fabric with a rubber band.

SOAP SCULPTURES

With this concoction you can quickly and easily make soap in beautiful shapes and colors that look like sculpted works of art.

WHAT YOU WILL NEED:

1 bar pure glycerin soap or Neutrogena bar soap
Candy mold or soap mold
Microwave-safe bowl

HOW TO CONCOCT IT:

1. Cut the bar of soap into 3 equal pieces.
2. Place the pieces of soap into a microwave-safe bowl.
3. Put the bowl in the microwave on high for 10 to 15 seconds and the soap will turn into liquid.
4. Remove the bowl with a potholder and quickly pour the melted soap into a candy mold or soap mold. Let your soap sit 30 minutes and then remove your Soap Sculptures from the mold.

CONCOCTION TIPS & IDEAS:

◆ This project requires assistance and supervision from an adult.
◆ Wrap Soap Sculptures in colored plastic wrap and place them in a decorated gift bag.

PETAL POTPOURRI

Mom will love this mixture of beautiful flower petals that will make any room smell good.

WHAT YOU WILL NEED:

2 cups flower petals (rose petals work best)
1/4 cup whole cloves
2 Tbs. salt
Small basket or bowl

HOW TO CONCOCT IT:

1. Put the petals in a large bowl.
2. Sprinkle salt and cloves over the petals and gently stir.
3. Place the mixture in a small basket or bowl and give as a gift along with an instruction card that states, "Stir once a day to keep your room smelling nice." (After a few days the petals will begin to dry, but they will look and smell fresh for months.)

CONCOCTION TIPS & IDEAS:

◆ Add some small pinecones and a couple of cinnamon sticks to your potpourri to make it smell and look even nicer.
◆ After the flower petals are completely dry, the potpourri can be stored in plastic ziplock bags or an airtight container.

QUILTED POT

Mother's will love this beautiful, easy-to-make pot that looks like a quilt.

WHAT YOU WILL NEED:
Scrap pieces of fabric cut into 2- to 3-inch squares
White glue
Terra-cotta pot
Paintbrush

HOW TO CONCOCT IT:
1. Paint a thin layer of white glue on the back of a fabric square and then stick it to the outside of the pot.
2. Repeat the above step several times until the entire outside of the pot is covered with fabric squares.
3. Let the pot dry overnight.

CONCOCTION TIPS & IDEAS:
◆ Plant a flower or plant in your pot and tie a ribbon around it before giving as a gift.
◆ To make the outside of the pot waterproof, apply several layers of clear spray shellac.

SAND BEADS

Make bead necklaces and bracelets similar to the beautiful ones worn by African women.

WHAT YOU WILL NEED:

1 cup sand
1/4 cup white glue
Toothpick
Yarn or string

HOW TO CONCOCT IT:

1. Mix sand and glue together in a small plastic bowl.
2. Knead the mixture until it is the consistency of a stiff dough. If the mixture is too moist, add more sand.
3. Pinch off a small piece of dough and roll it into the size of bead you want to make. Use a toothpick to make a hole in the middle of the bead big enough for your yarn or string to pass through.
4. Allow the beads to dry overnight or until hard.
5. Cut a piece of yarn or string to the desired size of the necklace or bracelet you want. String the beads and then tie your yarn or string together.

CONCOCTION TIPS & IDEAS:

◆ Make different colored beads by adding 1 Tbs. of poster paint or liquid tempera paint to the sand mixture before mixing.
◆ Sand Beads can also be decorated with paints and colored markers.

FATHER'S DAY

Father's Day became an official United States holiday in 1972. It was created to celebrate Fathers and express thanks to them for the important roles they have played in their children's lives.

Tips for making Father's Day special:

Make your Dad a special card telling him all the things you really like about him.

Make some coupons for Dad telling him you'll help with some of his chores. Some good ideas could be: I will help you wash the car; I will take out the trash today; I will help you work in the yard.

PET ROCK PAPERWEIGHT

Dad will love it when you give him your own version of this 1970s fad that took the country by storm.

WHAT YOU WILL NEED:

Clean round rock
Paint or colored markers
Google eyes
White glue

HOW TO CONCOCT IT:

1. Draw or paint a mouth, nose, and ears on your rock.
2. Use the white glue to apply the google eyes to your pet rock.
3. Let the rock dry overnight.

CONCOCTION TIPS & IDEAS:

◆ Use paper and colored markers to create a birth certificate for your pet rock. Be sure to include a
   name and birth date.
◆ Be creative and use other materials like feathers, sequins, and buttons to decorate your Pet Rock Paperweight.

MOSAIC MASTERPIECES

A great Father's Day gift! You'll be amazed how quick and easy it is to create these beautiful Mosaic Masterpieces.

WHAT YOU WILL NEED:

Plaster of Paris
Water
Assorted beads, buttons, marbles, stones, coins, or mosaic tiles
Small, shallow plastic dish

HOW TO CONCOCT IT:

1. Mix plaster of Paris and water together following the directions on the package.
2. Pour the plaster mixture into a small, shallow plastic dish, filling it half full. Let the plaster dry for a few minutes until it feels like a soft clay. Be careful not to let the plaster dry too long.
3. Quickly push the assorted beads, buttons, marbles, stones, coins, or mosaic tiles into the plaster to make pictures and designs.
4. Let your Mosaic Masterpiece dry overnight before trying to remove it from the dish.

CONCOCTION TIPS & IDEAS:

◆ Create a coaster by making your Mosaic Masterpiece in a small, round plastic dish. Glue a piece of felt on the bottom of the coaster to prevent it from scratching the furniture.

PUZZLE FRAMES

A unique and unusual Father's Day gift that will be cherished for years to come.

WHAT YOU WILL NEED:

Picture frame (flat frames work best)
White glue
Old puzzle pieces
Poster paint
Paintbrush

HOW TO CONCOCT IT:

1. Paint old puzzle pieces various colors using a paintbrush and poster paint. Make sure you have enough painted puzzle pieces to cover the front of your frame.
2. After the puzzle pieces have completely dried, lay the frame flat and use white glue to attach the puzzle pieces to the frame. Let the frame dry overnight.
3. Put a favorite picture of you and Dad in the frame and give it as a Father's Day gift.

CONCOCTION TIPS & IDEAS:

◆ Experiment by creating different types of frames decorated with other household objects like buttons, coins, etc.

INDEPENDENCE DAY

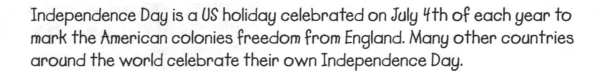

Independence Day is a US holiday celebrated on July 4th of each year to mark the American colonies freedom from England. Many other countries around the world celebrate their own Independence Day.

Tips for making your Independence Day even more fun:

Have a family barbeque or picnic. Serve red, white, and blue foods on colored plates.

Wear red, white, and blue clothing.

Attend a parade in your community or watch the fireworks together. Take along snacks and blankets to make it more festive.

FIRECRACKER PAINT PENS

They look like Independence Day firecrackers, but they are actually roll-on paint pens.

WHAT YOU WILL NEED:

Empty roll-on deodorant bottles
Liquid tempera paint or washable poster paint
Yellow, orange, and red construction paper
Tape or glue
String or yarn

HOW TO CONCOCT IT:

1. With the help of a parent, use a screwdriver to pop the roll-on ball out of the deodorant bottle.
2. Rinse out the bottle and fill it with liquid tempera paint or poster paint.
3. Snap the roll-on ball back into the bottle.
4. Use the construction paper and tape or glue to decorate the deodorant bottle like a firecracker and the bottle cap like a flame.

CONCOCTION TIPS & IDEAS:

◆ Add fine glitter to your Firecracker Paint Pen to create glitter paint.
◆ Decorate the paint pens to look like snowmen and use them to celebrate winter holidays.

TIE-DYED FLOWERS

These red, white, and blue Tie-Dyed Flowers will amaze your friends and family.

WHAT YOU WILL NEED:

Long-stemmed white carnation
Food coloring
Two 8 oz. glasses filled with water
Green thread

HOW TO CONCOCT IT:

1. Squeeze 7 to 8 drops of red food coloring in one glass of water and 7 to 8 drops of blue food coloring in the other glass of water.
2. Have an adult use a sharp knife and cut the stem of the carnation lengthwise making it into two thin stems.
3. Set the two glasses together. Place 1/2 of the carnation stem in the red water and the other half in the blue water.
4. After several hours the carnation should begin to be red, blue, and white. The longer the flower stays in the solution the brighter the color will be.
5. Remove the carnation from the food coloring solutions and wrap the stems back together with green thread. Place the carnation in a clear vase of water.

CONCOCTION TIPS & IDEAS:

◆ Make several different Tie-Dyed Flowers to create an entire bouquet.
◆ Make different colored flowers for other holidays.

PARTY CRACKERS

Party Crackers make great favors for Independence Day picnics and are sure to be a hit with children of all ages.

WHAT YOU WILL NEED:

Toilet paper tubes
Tissue paper, construction paper, or gift wrap
Colored markers, stickers, or poster paint
Candy, coins, marbles, small toys, etc.
Ribbon
Tape

HOW TO CONCOCT IT:

1. Tape one end of the toilet paper tube closed. Fill the tube with candy, coins, marbles, small toys, or anything else that will fit. Tape the other end of the tube shut.
2. Wrap the tube with tissue paper and then tie the ends with ribbon. Construction paper or gift wrap can also be used.
3. Decorate the outside of the tube with markers, stickers, or poster paint.
4. When you finish your picnic, distribute your Party Crackers. Each person pulls hard on both ends of their Party Crackers to open it.

CONCOCTION TIPS & IDEAS:

◆ Party Crackers also make great favors for birthday parties, Christmas, Hanukkah, or harvest festivals.

FIREWORKS PAINT

Create beautiful sheets of paper painted with patterns similar to fireworks.

WHAT YOU WILL NEED:

Marbles
Poster paint or liquid tempera paint
Plastic cups
Large shallow pan or pie tin
Paper

HOW TO CONCOCT IT:

1. Pour paint into the plastic cups.
2. Gently drop 3 to 4 marbles into the paint.
3. Place a sheet of paper flat on the bottom of the pan.
4. Spoon out the paint covered marbles from the plastic cup and into the pan.
5. Tilt the pan side to side to create Fireworks Paint designs. Repeat the above steps 1 to 3 more times using different colors of paint. Let the paint completely dry before handling the paper.

CONCOCTION TIPS & IDEAS:

◆ Use Fireworks Paint to create paper airplanes, place mats, greeting cards, or wrapping paper.

GRANDPARENT'S DAY

This holiday was created to honor and give thanks to our grandparents for all they have done to enrich our lives.

Tips for making Grandparent's Day special:

Giving your grandparents a current photograph is always a welcome treat.

Create a photo scrapbook of you with your grandparents throughout the year.

Make a scrapbook of artwork and poetry you have created.

Make a special gift with all the grandchildren's handprints. You can use fabric paint to press all the handprints on a tablecloth, shirt, or smooth watercolor paper. Or use a fabric marker to outline all the hands on a sweatshirt. Be sure to add the names with a fabric marker. This will be a forever keepsake.

GRANDPARENT'S WALK OF FAME STONE

Create a Walk of Fame Stone Grandma and Grandpa can put in their backyard, just like the one in Hollywood.

WHAT YOU WILL NEED:
Old bucket
8 cups quick-setting cement
Water
Shallow disposable cardboard box (11 x 16 works best)
Aluminum cake pan or large, round plant saucer
Stick (or wooden spoon)
Old ruler

HOW TO CONCOCT IT:
1. Mix cement and 2 cups of water together in a bucket until the mixture is the consistency of oatmeal. Add more cement or water if necessary.
2. Pour the mixture evenly into the cardboard box, aluminum cake pan, or large plant saucer. Your cement should be at least 1 1/2 to 2 inches thick.
3. Take an old ruler and rake across the top of the cement until smooth. Wait 2 to 5 minutes.
4. Place your hands or feet into the wet cement and push down 1 to 2 inches to make your impression. Immediately rinse your hands or feet with water.
5. Use a stick to write your name, age, and date in the cement.
6. Let the cement dry 48 hours. Then tear away the cardboard box. Give your Walk of Fame Stone to your grandparents for their backyard or garden.

CONCOCTION TIPS & IDEAS:
◆ Personalize your Walk of Fame Stone by adding seashells, toy cars, marbles, coins, dominoes, old jewelry, etc.

GLITTER CANDLES

Your grandparents will be amazed by these one-of-a-kind Glitter Candles.

WHAT YOU WILL NEED:

Pillar candle
White glue
Paintbrush
Glitter or sequins

HOW TO CONCOCT IT:

1. Paint the sides of the pillar candle with a thin layer of white glue.
2. Sprinkle the sides of the candle with glitter or sequins until completely covered.
3. Let the candle dry overnight before handling it.

CONCOCTION TIPS & IDEAS:

◆ Glitter Candles can be made for any holiday or occasion.
◆ Try decorating the sides of a candle with nontoxic paint and colored markers.

SPARKLE VOTIVES

Grandma and Grandpa will love these sparkling votives made from just a few household items.

WHAT YOU WILL NEED:
Baby food jar (clean with the label removed)
White glue
Paintbrush
Salt
Small picture or stickers

HOW TO CONCOCT IT:
1. Paint a thin layer of glue on the back of your picture and stick it on the outside of the baby food jar.
2. Paint over the picture and the outside of the jar with a thin layer of white glue.
3. Sprinkle a generous amount of salt over the wet glue on the outside of the jar.
4. Let the jar dry overnight, then place a tea light or small candle inside of the jar.

CONCOCTION TIPS & IDEAS:
◆ Create Sparkle Votives for other holidays by cutting pictures out of old holiday greeting cards and magazines.

MAGIC FLOWER STATIONERY

Transfer the image of real flowers onto paper and create beautiful stationery, envelopes, and greeting cards.

WHAT YOU WILL NEED:

Rubber mallet or hammer
Plastic wrap
Fresh flowers (pansies, impatiens, and geraniums work best)
Paper
Envelopes

HOW TO CONCOCT IT:

1. Arrange flowers face down on a sheet of paper in a border pattern.
2. Carefully cover the flowers with a sheet of clear plastic wrap.
3. Gently hit the flowers with the rubber mallet, being careful not to miss any parts of the flower.
4. Remove the plastic wrap and flowers from the paper to reveal your Magic Flower Stationery.

CONCOCTION TIPS & IDEAS:

◆ Use Magic Flower method to make custom greeting cards and invitations.
◆ Use Magic Flower method to decorate paper napkins and place mats for your next picnic.

HARVEST FESTIVAL

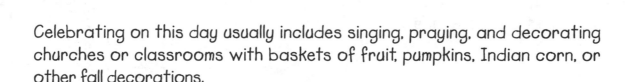

Celebrating on this day usually includes singing, praying, and decorating churches or classrooms with baskets of fruit, pumpkins, Indian corn, or other fall decorations.

In some churches people bring in food from home. The food is later distributed among the poor and the senior citizens.

Tips for a fun Harvest:

Plan a harvest feast for your own family.

Create paper place mats for the dinner table, decorated with cutouts and drawings of fruit and words of thanks.

HARVEST RAIN STICK

Children will have fun mixing seeds, beans, and rice together to create the sounds of a harvest rain shower.

WHAT YOU WILL NEED:

Heavy cardboard mailing tube
2 plastic caps or duct tape to seal the tube
Nails
Adhesive-backed shelf paper
Hammer
Seeds, rice, and dried beans

HOW TO CONCOCT IT:

1. Have an adult hammer nails into the mailing tube about 1/8-inch apart using the spiral seam of the cardboard tube as a guide.
2. Add several handfuls of assorted rice, seeds, and beans.
3. Seal each end of the tube securely with plastic caps or duct tape.
4. Decorate your Harvest Rain Stick with ribbon, paint, adhesive-backed shelf paper, wrapping paper, or fabric.

CONCOCTION TIPS & IDEAS:

◆ Use your Harvest Rain Stick as a musical instrument. Shake it and twist it to create a wide variety of different sounds.
◆ Decorate your Harvest Rain Stick by gluing seeds and beans on it in different patterns.

GOOFY GLOWING GUNK

This slimy, stretchy, gooey recipe has become one of the most popular concoctions of all time.

WHAT YOU WILL NEED:

Solution A
- 1 cup water
- 1 cup white glue
- 2 Tbs. poster paint

Solution B
- 1-1/3 cup warm water
- 4 Tbs. Borax laundry booster

HOW TO CONCOCT IT:

1. Mix ingredients in Solution A together in a medium bowl.
2. In a second bowl, mix the ingredients in Solution B.
3. Slowly pour Solution A into Solution B. (Do not mix!)
4. Roll Solution A around in Solution B 4 to 5 times, while gently kneading.
5. Lift Solution A out of Solution B and knead for 2 to 3 minutes.
6. Store Goofy Glowing Gunk in an airtight container or a plastic ziplock bag.

CONCOCTION TIPS & IDEAS:

◆ Add 8 to 12 drops of food coloring instead of Glow paint to the mixture to create Gunk in different colors.

GELATIN ORANGES

These tasty treats look like real orange wedges and make the perfect low-fat snack.

WHAT YOU WILL NEED:

Oranges
1 box orange flavored gelatin

HOW TO CONCOCT IT:

1. Have an adult cut the oranges in half and scoop out the center leaving only the outer skin.
2. Prepare the orange gelatin by following the instructions printed on the package.
3. Instead of pouring the liquid gelatin into a bowl to gel, pour it into the orange halves.
4. Place the orange halves full of gelatin mix into the refrigerator to harden for eight hours.
5. Remove the orange halves from the refrigerator and have an adult cut the oranges into wedges.

CONCOCTION TIPS & IDEAS:

◆ Use different types of citrus fruit (grapefruit, lemons, limes) along with different flavors of gelatin to create unique tasty treats.
◆ Follow the directions on the package of orange gelatin, except try substituting orange juice in place of water to create Gelatin Oranges bursting with flavor.

PRINCESS & PIRATE MAKEUP

Transform yourself into a prince or princess or any assortment of other characters with this wonderful face paint.

WHAT YOU WILL NEED:

2 Tbs. solid shortening
1 Tbs. cornstarch
Food coloring
Small make-up sponges

HOW TO CONCOCT IT:

1. Mix shortening and cornstarch together in a small bowl until smooth.
2. Add 4 to 6 drops of food coloring or Kid Concoctions Liquid color. Mix until the color is evenly blended.
3. Apply makeup to the face using a small make-up sponge.
4. Remove makeup with soap and water.

CONCOCTION TIPS & IDEAS:

◆ Add 1/2 tsp. of glitter to the makeup to make it sparkle.
◆ Try applying the makeup to your arms and hands for an even more complete character look.

THANKSGIVING

In the United States, Thanksgiving is one of the oldest and most widespread celebrations. This American holiday commemorates a harvest celebration held by the Pilgrims of Plymouth colony in 1621. There are also Thanksgiving holidays celebrated every year in Canada, Japan, South Korea, the Philippines, Puerto Rico, and the Virgin Islands.

Tips for making Thanksgiving a great holiday:

Give each family member an equal amount of dried beans, dried seed, or even pennies. Pass around a cup and each person puts one of their beans in the cup and tells everyone one thing that they are thankful for on this Thanksgiving. Keep passing the cup around until everyone has placed all their beans in the cup. We do this each year in our family and it is one of our favorite traditions.

Decorate your house with handmade decorations from the season like turkeys, pumpkins, pilgrim hats, or Indian corn.

PUMPKIN CANDLEHOLDERS

Use small pumpkins to create beautiful candleholders for your Thanksgiving dinner.

WHAT YOU WILL NEED:

2 small pumpkins
Knife
2 taper candles

HOW TO CONCOCT IT:

1. Have an adult use a knife to cut a hole in the top center of a small pumpkin. Make sure the hole is slightly smaller than the diameter of the candle you are using.
2. Push the candle into the center of the pumpkin. Make sure the candle is as straight as possible.

CONCOCTION TIPS & IDEAS:

◆ Try using red, green, or yellow apples, instead of small pumpkins, to create holiday candleholders.
◆ Create an even more festive look by decorating your Pumpkin Candleholders with colored markers or poster paint.

INDIAN CORN JEWELRY

Indian Corn Jewelry is easy to make and has the look of polished stone jewelry.

WHAT YOU WILL NEED:

1/2 cup dried Indian corn kernels
Sewing needle
Thread
Small bowl
Water

HOW TO CONCOCT IT:

1. Pour corn kernels into a small bowl of water.
2. Let the corn kernels soak overnight in the water or until soft.
3. Thread the needle, tying a knot at the end of the thread.
4. Have an adult push the needle through each soft kernel of corn until the necklace or bracelet is as long as you want it to be. Tie both ends of the thread together.

CONCOCTION TIPS & IDEAS:

◆ Try using dried sunflower seeds and yellow corn kernels along with the Indian corn to create even more beautiful bracelets and necklaces.

INDIAN NAPKIN RINGS

Use household items to create these wonderful napkin rings that look like an Indian's headband.

WHAT YOU WILL NEED:

Paper towel tubes
Construction paper
White glue
Scissors
Colored markers

HOW TO CONCOCT IT:

1. Cut a 3/4-inch wide circle from the paper towel tube. This will serve as the base of your napkin ring.
2. Use colored markers to draw a Native American design on your napkin ring so it looks like an Indian headband.
3. Cut small feathers from construction paper and fringe each side with scissors.
4. Put a drop of glue on the bottom of the feather and attach it to the inside of the napkin ring. After the glue is dry, roll up a napkin and slide your napkin ring over it.

CONCOCTION TIPS & IDEAS:

◆ Make fancy Indian Napkin Rings by gluing scraps of fabric over the napkin ring and using real feathers.

HANUKKAH

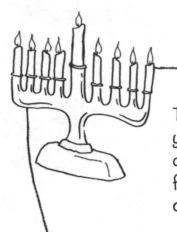

This Jewish holiday has been celebrated continuously for thousands of years by Jews all over the world. *Hanukkah*, the Jewish festival of lights, celebrates the rededication of the Jerusalem temple. During this eight-day festival, led by Judas Maccabaeus, oil lamps containing only enough oil for one night miraculously burned for eight nights.

Tips for making *Hanukkah* special:

Have a traditional *Latkes* meal, which is potato pancakes served with applesauce.

Make little *Gelt* bags of chocolate coins or money coins.

Plan special events as a family for each of the eight days of *Hanukkah*.

The Ultimate Book of Holiday Kid Concoctions

HANUKKAH PRETZEL STICKS

These tasty chocolate-covered pretzel sticks make the perfect Hanukkah snack.

WHAT YOU WILL NEED:

1 cup white chocolate chips
Pretzel rods
Blue candy sprinkles
Microwave-safe bowl
Wax paper

HOW TO CONCOCT IT:

1. Pour chocolate chips into a microwave-safe bowl and place in the microwave for 3 minutes or until melted. Have an adult remove the chocolate from the microwave and stir.
2. Use a spoon to drizzle the chocolate over 1/2 of the pretzel rod and then sprinkle with blue candy sprinkles.
3. Set the pretzel rods on wax paper for 30 minutes or until the chocolate has hardened.

CONCOCTION TIPS & IDEAS:

◆ Use different types of candy or crushed nuts to create pretzel sticks for other holidays and special occasions.
◆ Try making pretzel sticks using milk chocolate chips or peanut butter chips.

HANUKKAH ART RUBBINGS

Using this age-old rubbing technique, children can create beautiful Hanukkah art and designs.

WHAT YOU WILL NEED:

White glue
Cardboard
Paper
Crayons with the paper removed
Pencil

HOW TO CONCOCT IT:

1. Use a pencil to draw different Hanukkah symbols like a Star of David, *menorrah*, or *dreidel* on the cardboard.
2. Trace your design with the white glue.
3. Let the glue dry until hard.
4. Place a sheet of paper over the glue drawing and rub the paper with a crayon held in the horizontal position. The image of your glue drawing will appear on the paper.

CONCOCTION TIPS & IDEAS:

◆ Use Hanukkah Art Rubbings to create cards, wrapping paper, and pictures to celebrate this wonderful holiday.
◆ Create different looks by using assorted colors of crayons and paper.
◆ Use the same technique to create rubbings for lots of other holidays such as Christmas and Easter.

STAR OF DAVID SUGAR SCULPTURES

Create sparkling sugar sculptures using a few easy-to-find kitchen ingredients.

WHAT YOU WILL NEED:

1/2 cup sugar
1 tsp. glitter
1 tsp. water
Star of David cookie cutter

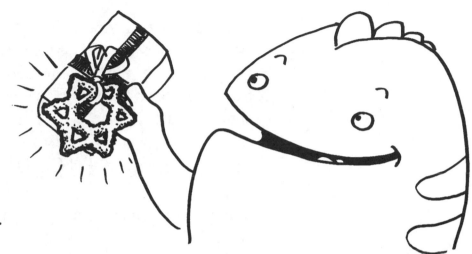

HOW TO CONCOCT IT:

1. Mix the sugar, glitter, and water together in a small bowl.
2. Press the sugar mixture into the cookie cutter.
3. Tap the cookie cutter gently onto a plate until the sugar sculpture pops out of the cookie cutter.
4. Let the sugar sculptures dry overnight before handling.

CONCOCTION TIPS & IDEAS:

◆ Glue a loop of yarn onto the back of your sculpture to create pretty package ties and ornaments.

◆ Add a few drops of food coloring to the sugar mixture to make sugar sculptures in an assortment of different colors.

◆ Use the same techniques with different cookie cutters to create sugar sculptures for other holidays.

CHRISTMAS

The word Christmas comes from the Old English term *Cristes maesse,* meaning "Christ's mass." This worship service was first held on December 25th to celebrate the birth of Jesus. Today, Christmas is celebrated by Christians around the world through worship and the custom of exchanging gifts.

Tips for a wonderful Christmas holiday:

Decorate a gingerbread house or make Christmas cookies together as a family.

Play Christmas music and sing along as you decorate your Christmas tree and home for the holiday.

Go carolling in your neighborhood with family and friends.

Give homemade gifts or cards to friends and family .

Adopt a family or person through a local church or community program and buy a Christmas gift for them. Sometimes this is the only way these people will receive a gift, and it is a great way to share the Christmas spirit.

SNOW IN A BOTTLE SNOW GLOBE

Enjoy the magic of a winter wonderland during the Christmas season and all year around with this classic Snow in a Bottle Snow Globe concoction.

WHAT YOU WILL NEED:

1 medium-sized baby food jar with lid (clean with the label removed)
White glitter
Glue gun
Small plastic figure or decorations
Cold water

HOW TO CONCOCT IT:

1. Using a glue gun, attach the plastic figure or decorations to the inside of the jar lid.
2. Fill the jar 1/2-inch from the top with cold water.
3. Add glitter.
4. Screw lid on the jar; turn it upside down and shake.

CONCOCTION TIPS & IDEAS:

◆ Use ribbon, garland, or plastic greenery to decorate the base of your Snow in a Bottle Snow Globe.
◆ Add 2 drops of food coloring to the water in the Snow in a Bottle Snow Globe to create a colorful winter sky.

GUMDROP ORNAMENTS

These pretty Christmas tree ornaments not only look great but taste pretty good too.

WHAT YOU WILL NEED:

Small round foam ball
Toothpicks
Gumdrops
String

HOW TO CONCOCT IT:

1. Push 3 gumdrops onto a toothpick leaving one end of the toothpick exposed.
2. Push the exposed end of the toothpick into foam ball. Repeat the above steps several times, until you have made enough gumdrop toothpicks to cover the entire ball.
3. Tie a string around the Gumdrop Ornament and hang it on your Christmas tree.

CONCOCTION TIPS & IDEAS:

◆ Make unique ornaments by arranging different color gumdrops in various patterns on the foam ball.

CHRISTMAS CANDY WREATHS

Christmas Candy Wreaths are not only very tasty, but they also make great Christmas tree ornaments and package ties.

WHAT YOU WILL NEED:

Bag of round peppermint discs
Small aluminum pie tins
Cookie sheet
Ribbon

HOW TO CONCOCT IT:

1. Arrange peppermint discs in a circle in the pie tins, making sure the discs are touching each other. Place on a cookie sheet.
2. Place cookie sheet in a preheated oven at 250 degrees for 3 to 5 minutes or until the peppermint discs melt together.
3. Have an adult help you remove the cookie sheet from the oven and let the candy wreaths cool for 15 minutes.
4. Use a spatula to carefully remove the cooled candy wreaths from the pie tins.
5. Use ribbon to tie a bow around the top of the candy wreaths.

CONCOCTION TIPS & IDEAS:

◆ Use red, white, and green peppermint candies to create a multicolored Christmas Candy Wreath.

CHOCOLATE FUDGE COCOA

This has been a favorite Christmas Eve drink in our family for years. Made with three kinds of chocolate, it's a chocolate lover's dream come true.

WHAT YOU WILL NEED:

1/2 gallon white milk
2/3 cup milk chocolate chips
6 Tbs. cocoa powder
1/3 cup sugar
1 quart chocolate milk

HOW TO CONCOCT IT:

1. Mix 1 cup of white milk, chocolate chips, cocoa, and sugar together in a large saucepan. Cook over low heat until the sugar dissolves.
2. Add the rest of the white milk and all of the chocolate milk. Stir the mixture until it begins to steam. Do not let the cocoa boil!
3. Pour into cups and serve. If cocoa is too hot, let it cool before drinking. Makes 12 servings.

CONCOCTION TIPS & IDEAS:

◆ This project requires help and supervision from an adult.
◆ Top your Chocolate Fudge Cocoa with miniature marshmallows or fresh whipped cream.
◆ When visiting friends or family during the holidays, take them a thermos full of Chocolate Fudge Cocoa with a gift tag attached containing the recipe.

CHRISTMAS POMANDER BALL

This old-fashioned holiday air freshener has always been one of our family favorites.

WHAT YOU WILL NEED:

1 orange
Whole cloves
1/4 cup cinnamon
Plastic ziplock bag
Ribbon
String

HOW TO CONCOCT IT:

1. Push the pointed end of the whole cloves into the orange
   one at a time until the entire orange is covered with cloves.
2. Pour the cinnamon into the ziplock bag. Place the orange in the bag and shake.
   Remove the orange from the bag and tie a piece of ribbon around the orange.
3. Tie a second piece of ribbon around the orange so it crisscrosses the first ribbon at the bottom.
   Tie a knot at the top.
4. Tie a piece of string around the knotted ribbons. This will serve as a hanger for your Christmas Pomander Ball.
5. The orange will eventually shrink and become rock hard. You can enjoy your Pomander Ball for many years to come.

CONCOCTION TIPS & IDEAS:

◆ You can create a beautiful pomander arrangement by making several pomanders, trying different colors of ribbon
   around each one, and arranging them in a clear glass bowl.
◆ Use your Pomander Ball as a Christmas tree ornament or wrap it in a piece of netting and give it as a gift.

MINI LANTERNS

These unique lanterns will bring lots of holiday cheer to any Christmas celebration.

WHAT YOU WILL NEED:
Soup can (clean with the label removed)
Hammer
Nail
Paper
Votive candle

HOW TO CONCOCT IT:
1. Fill the soup can with water and place in the freezer for 24 hours or until frozen solid.
2. Cut a piece of paper the same height as the can and long enough to be wrapped around the can.
3. Use a pencil to draw a simple holiday design on the paper (e.g., Christmas tree, snowman, snowflake).
4. When the water is completely frozen, remove the can from the freezer and wrap the paper around the can securing it with a piece of tape.
5. Lay the can on a thick folded towel and ask an adult to help you use the hammer and nail to punch holes along the lines of your design.
6. Place the can in warm water until the ice is melted. Have an adult place a votive candle in the can.

CONCOCTION TIPS & IDEAS:
◆ Place Mini Lanterns on each side of your front door or along a driveway or front walkway.
◆ Mini Lanterns can also be made for other occassions such as birthdays or fall festivals.

APPLESAUCE-CINNAMON ORNAMENTS

This extremely fragrant dough has a very unique texture.

WHAT YOU WILL NEED:

1/2 cup cinnamon
1/2 cup applesauce
Plastic ziplock bag
Drinking straw
Ribbon

HOW TO CONCOCT IT:

1. Pour cinnamon and applesauce into a ziplock bag.
2. Seal the ziplock bag and knead until the mixture turns to dough.
3. Roll the dough out about 1/4-inch thick. Cut different holiday shapes out of the dough, using Christmas cookie cutters.
4. Make a small hole toward the top of your ornament using a drinking straw.
5. Let your Applesauce-Cinnamon Ornaments air-dry for 12 hours or until hard. Tie a piece of ribbon through the hole in each ornament and hang them on the Christmas tree.

CONCOCTION TIPS & IDEAS:

◆ Applesauce-Cinnamon Ornaments also make great package decorations and holiday air fresheners.

MAGIC REINDEER FOOD

Our children always have fun making this magic food for Santa's reindeer.

WHAT YOU WILL NEED:

1/2 cup dry oats
1/4 cup dry cereal
1 Tbs. brown sugar
1 Tbs. nuts or candy sprinkles

HOW TO CONCOCT IT:

1. Mix all of the ingredients in a small bowl and stir.
2. Sprinkle Magic Reindeer Food outside around your house on Christmas Eve.
3. Since the Reindeer Food is magic, Santa's reindeer will only need to eat a little bit. They always seem to leave some food behind for their other animal friends.

CONCOCTION TIPS & IDEAS:

◆ Place Magic Reindeer Food in a plastic ziplock bag and tie a red ribbon around the top. This is a great gift to give during the Christmas season.
◆ Leave Santa some milk and cookies on your kitchen table along with a note letting him know you left Magic Reindeer Food outside for his friends.

BIRTHDAY

Your Birthday is the anniversary of the day you were born. Although no one knows for sure when Birthday celebrations first began, we do know that Birthdays have been celebrated since the early fourteenth century.

Tips for a great Birthday:

Throw your own Kid Concoctions birthday party. Make some of your favorite concoctions at the party.

Make Treasure Stones (recipe on page 75) and hide them around your yard or house. Have a Treasure Stone hunt at your party.

Have your party guests make their own ice cream with the Kid Concoction Shake & Make Ice Cream recipe found on page 76.

Make your own goody bags or gifts to give as party favors.

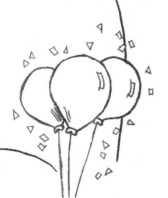

EDIBLE BIRTHDAY CARD

Why give a regular paper birthday card when you can give this easy-to-make Edible Card.

WHAT YOU WILL NEED:

1 package premade sugar cookie dough
1 beaten egg yolk
Cookie sheet
Food coloring
Small paintbrushes

HOW TO CONCOCT IT:

1. Mix the egg yolk and 3 to 4 drops of food coloring together in a small bowl. Repeat this process several times to make different colors of paint.
2. Roll the cookie dough out on a greased cookie sheet.
3. Cut and shape the dough to the size card desired.
4. Use the small paintbrushes and the egg yolk/food coloring mixture to write a message and paint a design on the card.
5. Ask an adult to help you bake as directed on the package of cookie dough.

CONCOCTION TIPS & IDEAS:

◆ Add pizzazz to your Edible Birthday Card by sprinkling it with candy sprinkles or colored sugar before baking.
◆ Wrap your Edible Birthday Card with color plastic wrap and tie a ribbon around it.

TREASURE STONES

Our most popular concoction ever! Small stones your party guests can break open to reveal hidden treasures and secret birthday messages.

WHAT YOU WILL NEED:

1 cup flour
1 cup used coffee grounds
1/2 cup salt
1/4 cup sand
3/4 cup water

HOW TO CONCOCT IT:

1. Mix all dry ingredients together in a medium bowl.
2. Slowly add water and knead until the mixture is the consistency of bread dough. If the mixture is too wet, add more flour.
3. Break off pieces of dough and roll them into the size of baseballs.
4. Make a hole in the center of the balls big enough to hide treasures in.
5. Fill the holes with treasures and seal them with some extra dough.
6. Let your Treasure Stones air-dry for 2 to 3 days (until hard), or bake in the oven on a cookie sheet at 150 degrees for 15 to 20 minutes. (Due to low temperatures, treasures inside the stones will not melt.)
7. This recipe makes 2 large, 3 medium, or 4 small Treasure Stones.

CONCOCTION TIPS & IDEAS:

◆ Hide Treasure Stones in your backyard to have the ultimate birthday party treasure hunt.
◆ You can use plastic or metal jewelry, plastic or metal charms, small plastic toys, erasers, plastic or metal coins, balloons, and candy inside your Treasure Stones.

SHAKE & MAKE ICE CREAM

You and your party guests can make delicious creamy ice cream in just minutes.

WHAT YOU WILL NEED:

2 Tbs. sugar
1 cup half-and-half
1/2 tsp. vanilla extract
6 Tbs. rock salt
1 pint-size plastic ziplock bag
1 gallon-size plastic ziplock bag
Crushed ice

HOW TO CONCOCT IT:

1. Combine the sugar, half-and-half and vanilla in the pint-size
   ziplock bag and seal.
2. Fill the gallon-size ziplock bag 1/2 full with crushed ice. Add the rock salt.
3. Place the sealed, pint-size ziplock bag into the gallon-size ziplock bag and seal.
4. Shake the gallon-size bag for 5 to 7 minutes or until the ice cream hardens.
5. Open the small ziplock bag and enjoy!

CONCOCTION TIPS & IDEAS:

◆ Make chocolate ice cream by adding 2 Tbs. of chocolate syrup to the ice cream mixture before shaking.
◆ Try topping your ice cream with sprinkles, nuts, or fresh fruit.

SLIME & WORM DESSERT

This yummy treat is sure to add excitement to any birthday party.

WHAT YOU WILL NEED:

1 cup premade vanilla pudding
Green food coloring
Gummy worms
2 crushed vanilla wafers

HOW TO CONCOCT IT:

1. Mix pudding and 3 to 4 drops of green food coloring together in a small bowl until well-blended.
2. Spoon the pudding into a small dessert dish.
3. Sprinkle the top of the pudding with the crushed vanilla wafers.
4. Add gummy worms and serve.

CONCOCTION TIPS & IDEAS:

◆ Use red food coloring instead of green and omit the gummy worms to create a Lava or Volcano Dessert.

BIRTHDAY CAKE COOKIES

These wonderful cookies are easy to make and taste just like a birthday cake.

WHAT YOU WILL NEED:

1 box cake mix
2 eggs
1/2 cup vegetable oil
Nuts & chocolate chips (optional)
Cookie sheet

HOW TO CONCOCT IT:

1. Mix oil, eggs, and cake mix together in a large bowl.
2. Stir in chocolate chips and nuts.
3. Drop tablespoon-sized mounds of batter onto a greased cookie sheet.
4. Get an adult to help you bake in a preheated oven at 350 degrees for 10 minutes.

CONCOCTION TIPS & IDEAS:

◆ Experiment by using different flavors of cake mix.
◆ Decorate your Birthday Cake Cookies with frosting and candy sprinkles.

INDEX